The Benefit Package

30 days of God's goodness
from Psalm 103

CrossRiver
BREWSTER, KANSAS USA

For more on Tamara Clymer, please visit TamaraClymer.com

Editor: Tamara Clymer
Proofreader: Debra L. Butterfield
Cover Art: © Anskuw | Dreamstime.com - Red Gift Box With White Bow Photo
Printed in the United States of America.

Contents

Provision

"Let all that I am praise the LORD; may I never forget the good things he does for me." — *Psalm 103:2*

Frozen Pipes

"Let all that I am praise the LORD; with my whole heart,
I will praise his holy name." — Psalm 103:1

A young, newly married couple in the mid-1970s, my husband and I lived in a small older house in west-central Missouri. While the dwelling was more than adequate for our needs, the antiquated plumbing couldn't withstand the subzero temperatures in the winter of 1976.

Many mornings we awoke to frozen and broken water pipes. On several occasions, the pipes were beyond repair and had to be replaced, involving hours of work in the cramped and muddy area underneath the house.

We learned a few tips from family and friends, like keeping the hot water faucet dripping just a little and leaving the cabinet doors open under the kitchen sink, to avoid the dreaded dilemma. But it didn't always work.

I clearly remember the bitterly cold and blustery winter evening when I returned from my job as a first-year teacher and realized there was no sound of water dripping. The inevitable had happened again.

I dreaded telling my new husband. I knew the pipes hadn't been frozen when he left for his second-shift job at the factory because he would have called me or left a note. When he got home, I broke the news. We went to bed late that night, disheartened and depressed, knowing there was nothing to be done. The pipes had been frozen for hours and the wind continued to blow while the temperature plummeted.

"Don't forget to pray about the pipes," Monty said to me as we turned out the lights.

"God doesn't have time to worry about our stupid pipes," I replied. Even though I only half-heartedly meant that, God saw it as a lesson in the making for two young newlyweds.

It was no sooner out of my mouth when we heard a gurgling noise coming from the kitchen. "Did you hear that?" I asked.

"It's only air in the lines."

Within five minutes, however, we learned otherwise as water gushed, full force, from the open kitchen faucets.

From an earthly perspective, it was impossible. From a heavenly perspective, though, our compassionate and loving heavenly Father had satisfied our desire with good things and taught us that nothing, absolutely nothing, is too difficult for Him!

Even though it has been more than thirty-five years since that cold January night, we have found God to be a faithful promise keeper, and we now know that nothing is too insignificant to discuss with Him. We have learned to make prayer our first priority, not our last resort.

- Barbara Gordon

"O Sovereign LORD! You made the heavens and earth by your strong hand and powerful arm. Nothing is too hard for you!" — Jeremiah 32:17

Prayer

Lord Jesus, we so often underestimate Your great love and compassion for us. Increase our capacity to know how wide and long and high and deep Your love is toward us. Thank You for the lessons You teach us. May we be quick learners. Amen.

Peace by Piece

"Let all that I am praise the LORD; may I never forget the good things he does for me." — Psalm 103:2

P lease, Lord let him be wrong!"

I breathed a silent prayer as my husband headed to work that morning, hoping it would bring me peace. It didn't work. Instead, fear settled in the pit of my stomach.

Shad was worried. The last six months were tough. Pet owners cancelled elective surgeries and ranchers handled more of the cattle jobs on their own — all because of the sluggish economy. Often my husband, a veterinarian, had to search for things to do around the clinic just to keep busy.

He was convinced the afternoon meeting with his boss spelled doom. He was right. That night he came home carrying a box with his medical books and a severance check.

That's when the very carefully placed pieces of our life fell apart. Never in our nearly 25 years of married life had things been so bleak. Never.

Overnight fear crept in. And doubt — lots and lots of doubt. "God is in control," I told friends. "He has a plan for us," I reminded the kids. And I meant it. I knew He could take care of us. I just wasn't sure He would.

For weeks I struggled with my doubt — watching as the

bills piled up and the checking account dwindled. Time and time again I prayed for guidance, for relief, for provision…but never with a clear sense of confidence.

Then one day I tried something new. My dad, a former minister, told me to read the Psalms out loud to my heavenly Father. "Let Him know how you feel," he said. "If David, a man after God's own heart, could say these things to Him, so can you. You're the daughter of the Most High."

I grabbed my Bible and dug in, determined to find the toughest passage in Psalms. It didn't take long — there it was in chapter 22.

"My God, my God, why have you abandoned me?" I prayed out loud. "Why are you so far away when I groan for help? Every day I call to you, my God, but you do not answer. Every night you hear my voice, but I find no relief." (Ps. 22:1-2)

A few verses later, I was in tears. "Praise the Lord, all you who fear him! Honor him, all you descendants of Jacob! Show him reverence, all you descendants of Israel! For he has not ignored or belittled the suffering of the needy. He has not turned his back on them, but has listened to their cries for help.…The poor will eat and be satisfied. All who seek the Lord will praise him. Their hearts will rejoice with everlasting joy." (Ps. 22:23–24, 26)

I could almost feel the Lord wrap His arms around me. Slowly, one by one, He reminded me of a few things that had happened in the weeks leading up to Shad's layoff — a larger than expected tax return that let us pay off a few bills…a big freelance job dropped in my lap out of the blue…a refund check on an overpaid bill. God wasn't ignoring me! He was there all along — getting us ready for the tough road ahead.

I didn't hear an angelic chorus or see a beam of light from heaven. Instead, a quiet peace settled in my spirit. He did have a plan for us. He was in control. Our heavenly Father went to the trouble of preparing us ahead of time. He would provide for us now. I could rest in that.

Slowly, over the next few weeks we watched as God put the pieces of our life back together. While others waited in the unemployment line, Shad was offered a job within a few weeks. Instead of worrying when it didn't meet our financial needs, we prayed. A few days later they called, upping the offer and giving him permission to do consulting work.

Piece by piece God addressed every issue we came up with. By the time we loaded the moving van, He provided a way for us to leave — without incurring any debt.

A lot has changed in the last year. Not only has Shad changed jobs, we now live in a new town, the kids are in a different school and our lifestyle downsized. But most of importantly — I have no doubts. They're gone.

I know God not only can — He will. And I now say with confidence, "Now all glory to God, who is able, through his mighty power at work within us, to accomplish infinitely more than we might ask or think." (Eph. 3:20)

—Tamara Clymer

"Praise the LORD, all you who fear him! Honor him, all you descendants of Jacob! Show him reverence, all you descendants of Israel! For he has not ignored or belittled the suffering of the needy. He has not turned his back on them, but has listened to their cries for help. I will praise you in the great assembly. I will fulfill my vows in the presence of those who worship you.

The poor will eat and be satisfied. All who seek the LORD will praise him. Their hearts will rejoice with everlasting joy." — Psalm 22:23–26

❦

Prayer

Lord, when times get tough, remind me of all the times You have provided. Bring to my memory Your promises and Your proven faithfulness. Show me Your power and Your provision and give me the strength to trust You, even when things look bleak. Amen.

His Eye is on the Cardinal

"He fills my life with good things." — Psalm 103:5a

Male cardinals look brilliant perched among the dismal browns and tans of our fallow garden. Their antics, as they feed and bathe, prove our Father has a sense of humor. The sweetness of their songs is worth recording.

Two years ago, ahead of a huge snowstorm, I watched the males stand watch as the female cardinals burrowed along the fence and tree lines into piles of poplar leaves. Then they hung onto tree limbs through the blast of sixty-mile-an-hour winds and eight inches of snow.

As winds died back a day later, the females flew out of their hiding places and returned to protection with their mates. Frigid cold followed for more than a week and we didn't see any signs of them until the temperatures rose. They were well bunkered in the snow beds, complete with squash bugs to eat.

An avid bird watcher, I was surprised. I had never seen anything like it. Our Creator designed this little red bird with enough brain power to find protection from an approaching storm. While I know there is greater purpose, I like to think He did it, in part, because I enjoy the birds.

Jesus said that our heavenly Father looks after the sparrows. He loves us more than birds or any other creature because He made us in His image, which means He will provide for us too. He will show us the way as long as we listen and follow His instructions.

Take a moment to pay attention with your ears and your heart. It's easy when we get into the habit of hearing His voice. He's always talking and always listening.

– Deb Kemper

~♦♦♦♦♦♦~

"Look at the birds. They don't plant or harvest or store food in barns, for your heavenly Father feeds them. And aren't you far more valuable to him than they are?" — Matthew 6:26

~♦♦♦♦♦♦~

Prayer

Father, You are amazing in Your provision for us. Your mercy flows over us with every breath of air we draw into our lungs. Your grace abounds in us, through the design of our bodies and minds. You enable us to think, act, and carry out Your will. Thank You for loving us so much that You sent the best part of that love to redeem us. Amen.

Childlike Faith

"For he knows how weak we are;
he remembers we are only dust." — Psalm 103:14

I t was an easy pregnancy, and my daughter arrived into the world healthy and beautiful. I should have been a glowing new mom. Instead, I cried more than I smiled and felt gripping anxiety. My thoughts were unfocused, I had trouble sleeping, and emotionally I just couldn't enjoy being a mom.

Depression spanned four generations in my family. I spent much of my childhood ashamed of this illness' hold on my loved ones. When the lingering sadness and anxiety hit me as a new mom, I initially hid it from everyone around me. Depression was not going to destroy my life, as it had some of my relatives.

A few weeks after my daughter was born, a care package arrived from a longtime friend who lived too far away to visit. Her box was filled with baby clothes and books. One of the books had "Psalm 91" written on it. The illustrated picture book was intended for a child, but I couldn't take my eyes off it. Page by page, the story unfolded of how God protects us by covering us with His feathers. When we are afraid, the book promised God would provide a safe refuge.

I envisioned God in heaven as this enormous eagle spreading His wings in either direction as far as I could see, watching over me as I struggled with inner turmoil. How could He do that?

One night as I couldn't fall asleep yet again, the words of Psalm 91:15 came to mind, via my own paraphrase: "(The young mom) will call on me, and I will answer (her); I will be with (her) in trouble, I will rescue and honor (her)."

"God," I prayed that night. "Help me."

I opened my Bible and lay my head on its pages, too exhausted to read. I felt like a child once again — ashamed, afraid, and lost. I wanted God to reach out His heavenly arms and hold me.

The next morning was my daughter's well-baby checkup. When I casually mentioned to the doctor, "I think I'm depressed," she offered support in the form of prescription antidepressant medication.

A few days later, I reached out to other moms in my neighborhood. We got together over coffee and shared how difficult it was, at times, to care for our children. One mom confided she also dealt with depression.

Within a couple of weeks, I found the strength to drag myself and my daughter to church on Sunday. As I listened to the worship songs, I felt something stir deep within me. It was the need to sing to God. It was a desire to thank Him for helping me.

I closed my eyes and sang as I held my daughter close to my chest. With each song, waves of peace flowed through me and provided comfort.

As I held my innocent child, it felt as if God were wrapping His own arms around me. Just as he promised.

- Shanna Groves

⚜

"Those who live in the shelter of the Most High will find rest in the shadow of the Almighty." — Psalm 91:1

⚜

Prayer

When the storms hit my life, Lord, help me to come to You with a pure, childlike faith. Allow my humble actions to be a powerful example to others of who Jesus is. Thank You for modeling pure faith through Your Son. Amen.

Forgiveness

"He forgives all my sins…" — Psalm 103:3a

Caught in Barbed Wire

"He forgives all my sins..." — Psalm 103:3a

When I was a little girl living on our family farm, I often had to walk a couple of miles to my one-room schoolhouse. The shortest route included crossing a barnyard, climbing through a barbed wire fence, and plodding across a huge field. In the winter, when the field was full of snow, it was quite a challenge to hike through it in heavy rubber boots and bulky snow pants.

Returning home one wintry afternoon, I lifted the top wire of the fence, bent over, and put one leg over the lower wire. As I pulled the other leg through, the barbs caught on my snow pants. I tried to go back through the fence, but couldn't! And no matter what I did, I could not go forward either. I was trapped.

I yelled at the top of my lungs hoping to get my mother's attention, but she was in the house, busy with my younger sister and brothers and couldn't hear my frantic calls.

Cold and miserable, I sobbed as the shadows began to lengthen across the field. Finally, my mother noticed I was not home. She put on her coat, scarf, and boots and came to investigate. What a relief when she pulled the barbed wire from my pants and set me free!

Sin is like that barbed wire. It traps us and holds us prisoner, wrestle with it as we may. Benjamin Franklin revealed his own battle with character flaws as he revealed in his autobiography in a section called "Arriving at Moral Perfection." He listed thirteen virtues he wished to perfect by charting them each day. If he failed at one of the attributes, he gave himself a black mark.

Eventually, he admitted it was impossible to be perfect, but rationalized by saying in effect, "Oh, well, even if it were possible to conquer the traits, then I would have to struggle with the sin of pride at having been able to do so!"

Franklin's project reveals how limited human beings are at achieving righteousness through our own strength. We can't fully keep the law set out for us in the Ten Commandments and arrive at sinless and holy perfection. It's a terrible predicament because "the wages of sin is death." (Rom. 6:23) And no one is exempt because "everyone has sinned; we all fall short of God's glorious standard." (Rom. 3:23)

Try as we might, there is only one way to be released from sin and that is through accepting God's gift of salvation and confessing our sins. "If we confess our sins, He is faithful and just to forgive us *our* sins and to cleanse us from all unrighteousness." (1 John 1:9 NKJV)

We don't have to be caught forever in the barbed wire fence of sin. We can call to a loving Father, who will release us, forgive us, heal us, redeem us, and give us the gift of eternal life in Christ Jesus.

– *Marcia Schwartz*

"If we say that we have no sin, we deceive ourselves, and the truth is not in us. If we confess our sins, He is faithful and just to forgive us our sins and to cleanse us from all unrighteousness." — 1 John 1:8–9 (NKJV)

Prayer

O Holy God, I know I fall short of purity, goodness, and righteousness. I confess and acknowledge my sins and I ask You to save me from sin and death. I accept Your gift of salvation and ask You to crown me with Your love and compassion today and always. Amen.

A King Worth Fighting For

"He will not constantly accuse us,
nor remain angry forever." — Psalm 103:9

Who doesn't love a good adventure? As a kid, I certainly did. One summer, when I was only eight or nine, my friends and I built a ship. It was made of old corrugated cardboard and was the pride of four young pirates who fought gators, braved the fiercest storms, and took to the green seas of Camelot, all in defense of an imaginary king.

The cardboard box withstood quarreling best friends, cheating brothers and sisters, and competitions to see who could swing the highest on the swing set. By the time the hot summer days gave way to warm nights, our battles would end and my friends and I would lay on the top of the swing set and watch a fireworks show so close it rained down on us and seemed to celebrate our friendship.

Those fights, real and imaginary, at times seemed insurmountable. Often, after a big quarrel, my friend and I wouldn't speak to each other for days. One time, I even left my half of our best friend heart necklace on her front porch.

How silly it seems now as I reflect on that fight. My heart was broken — as broken as those two little golden hearts, or so I thought. Twenty years later, I have no idea what that fight was about. The battle is long since forgiven and forgotten.

What a great reminder of my relationship with my heavenly Father and true King of Kings. If my friend and I were so willing to forgive each other, how much more is God ready to forgive me for the sins I commit?

What King are you fighting for? Are you a part of His army on His mission? Or are you bogged down with the distractions and sins of this world? What mistakes have you made that you need to repent? He is there, ready and willing to offer forgiveness and to wipe your slate clean.

As children, my friends and I fought for an imaginary king. Today, I battle for the King of Kings — trusting in Him and His ways to be merciful and forgiving. It is the benefit of being a child of the Most High.

- Crystal Nichols

❦❦❦❦

"Whoever loves a pure heart and gracious speech will have the king as a friend." — Proverbs 22:11

❦❦❦❦

Prayer

Father, thank You for being my friend at all times. You have come to love me and teach me with grace and mercy. Forgive me for the mistakes I make, be my strength to turn from them. Amen

Hiss & Run

"He does not punish us for all our sins; he does not deal harshly with us, as we deserve." — Psalm 103:10

Our home was a battle ground.

Two months before we brought Lucy home, we adopted our German shepherd/golden retriever from a calm home where he enjoyed morning chases with the cat. Lucy, an orange tabby, came from the shelter after living on the streets where dogs must have been the supreme enemy.

Now, as they met for the first time, Ranger ran toward the carrier, sniffing at its occupant, hoping for a playmate. Lucy wanted nothing to do with him. While Ranger behaved like a perfect gentleman, Lucy hissed any time she saw him.

When she made the annoying sound, we isolated her in the bathroom for a few minutes. She eventually got the message that hissing was not allowed and gave Ranger a wide berth — only hissing when he was nearby.

We thought Lucy had put hissing behind her, but one day as they passed each other in the hall she turned and hissed again. Before I could call her name, she darted up the stairs and scooted into the bathroom all on her own.

How many times have I done the exact same thing? I try to live in a way that pleases God, then find myself in the middle of choices I regret. I quickly banish myself to the land of "I am such a horrible person because I messed up." I reject God's gift of forgiveness before He rejects me. But running from His gift is spitting in the face of the giver.

Imagine presenting someone with an expensive gift. You thought about it long and hard to find just the right thing. When you visit that person, instead of finding the object proudly displayed, it's in the garbage.

That's what spit feels like. Sometimes consequences remain even after forgiveness, like unkind words spoken in anger leave a mark even after an apology. Consequences serve to train us and should not be equated with lack of forgiveness.

"Since we respected our earthly fathers who disciplined us, shouldn't we submit even more to the discipline of the Father of our spirits, and live forever? For our earthly fathers disciplined us for a few years, doing the best they knew how. But God's discipline is always good for us, so that we might share in his holiness." (Heb. 12:9–10)

What if we don't deserve the forgiveness? None of us do. "But God showed his great love for us by sending Christ to die for us while we were still sinners." (Rom. 5:8)

In order to fully embrace His forgiveness, you need to trust Him. Look at His actions on the cross, in your own life, and in the life of those around you.

Choose to believe Him even when you don't feel like it. Take Him at His word and quit reminding God about what He has already forgotten.

Accept His gift. With the death of His Son, He has removed your sin from you as far as the east is from the west.

- Angela Meyer

~~~~~

"Since we respected our earthly fathers who disciplined us, shouldn't we submit even more to the discipline of the Father of our spirits, and live forever? For our earthly fathers disciplined us for a few years, doing the best they knew how. But God's discipline is always good for us, so that we might share in his holiness." — Hebrews 12:9–10

~~~~~

Prayer

Father, thank You for Your gift of forgiveness and grace that is mine just for the asking. I pray that You will help me to accept that gift and be willing to forgive myself. Help me to also remember that You have not only forgiven me, but You won't hold it against me and You will remember it no more. Amen.

The Letter

*"He has removed our sins as far from us
as the east is from the west." — Psalm 103:12*

M om, you were supposed to protect me."

A soft August breeze warmed my face as I sat out on the front deck of my home. I was searching for answers.

Five years had passed since my then thirteen-year-old daughter had first spoken those words to me. Still, they echoed in my mind, guilt piercing my thoughts like a bullet through my brain.

I couldn't understand why she was angrier at me than at her stepfather. He was the one who had sexually abused her. During those five years, she had run away so many times and done so many unspeakable things to hurt me, I lost count. Our relationship was so out of control the Department of Social Services (DSS) placed her in a foster home.

Now she was nearing eighteen, and DSS would soon release her from foster care. She would be on her own, working to forge out a life for herself. Would that life include me? Our relationship was strained at best — almost nonexistent. Time had healed only a few of our wounds. It seemed no matter how much prayer and effort I put into making things better, a wall of pain still divided us.

My heart ached over our broken relationship. Would God

ever bring reconciliation and restoration? I looked at the aspens in our yard quaking in the wind and beyond them at Pikes Peak as if expecting God to speak to me from the mountain as He had to Moses on Mount Sinai.

"God, what should I do?"

Apologize.

I bristled. What had I done wrong that I should apologize? I was the best parent I knew how to be. Still, if I was honest, I felt like a colossal failure. Admitting another mistake would seal the deal. Deep down I knew I had failed her. When she needed me, I wasn't there to stop her stepfather from hurting her. What was important was her perspective on my lack of action.

I didn't trust myself to say the right words over the phone, so I grabbed a piece of paper and a pencil. "Dear daughter, I'm sorry I wasn't there to protect you. Please forgive me." For the first time in a long time, I felt at peace.

A few days later, the phone rang.

"Mom, I got your letter."

I held my breath, expecting the usual argument. Instead, we talked for a long time and before the conversation was over we were both crying. God had opened the door to restoration.

If I had not set my pride aside that summer afternoon and asked my daughter to forgive me, our relationship may have never healed. At best, it would have taken years longer for the door to open. Forgiveness allowed healing to begin and restoration to occur.

King Solomon's proverbs tells us, "Love prospers when a fault is forgiven." (Prov. 17:9) Next to "I love you," the most important words we can speak to the people in our lives are, "Please forgive me." If I expect people who hurt me to say, "I'm sorry," then I need to be willing to do the same. God loves us with an unfailing love, and when we ask Him to forgive us, He does.

Today, twelve years later, my daughter and I are as close as any mother and daughter can be. Perhaps even closer because of the struggles we have shared.

Are there people in your life whom you have wounded? Please consider asking God for the strength and opportunity to ask for their forgiveness. Restoration is worth it.

- Debra L. Butterfield

~~~~~

"Love prospers when a fault is forgiven, but dwelling on it separates close friends." — Proverbs 17:9

~~~~~

Prayer

Father, please open my eyes to those in my life whom I have hurt, whether I intended the pain or not. Give me the courage and the opportunity to ask for their forgiveness. For those who have hurt me in the past, give me the strength to forgive them, regardless of whether they request it. Amen.

Love

"For his unfailing love toward those who fear him is as great as the height of the heavens above the earth." — Psalm 103:11

Tiara Power

"…and crowns me with love and tender mercies." — Psalm 103:4b

*R*ejection, betrayal, disaster — nouns that described my life.

After twenty-five years of marriage to my best friend, all my legal documents now read *divorced* in the marital status box. Besides the obvious emotional trauma, I found myself trying to find a new identity in my fifties. Who was I supposed to be in this decade of life and how could I possibly fulfill God's plan as a divorced minister?

"This wasn't supposed to be my life, God," I complained.

He pointed me to Psalm 103. One of His defined benefits included crowning me with steadfast love and mercy.

"Humph," I growled as I stared in the mirror at the bags under my eyes. "I do not look or feel like anything royal. Crowned with love and mercy? What does that mean?"

But I could not dismiss the idea of a crown from my mind. So I did what any disgruntled minister does when searching for the meaning of some spiritual concept. I thumbed through my concordance for *crown* words.

The answer played peekaboo with me, sandwiched in the middle of the beautiful poetry of Isaiah. The prophet speaks of the mission of Jesus and how He binds up the brokenhearted, surely including those whose lives have been shattered by divorce. One of the ways He comforts the brokenhearted is to "give a crown of beauty for ashes." (Isa. 61:3)

A crown of beauty. A beautiful crown.

So to help myself remember Isaiah's words and the promises of God, I drove to the party store and bought a tiara. No diamonds, just a plastic replica with sparkly rhinestones and a comfy comb to keep it on my head. Then I drove home, repeating Isaiah 61:3, "A crown of beauty instead of ashes…a crown of beauty…in God's eyes I am beautiful…crowned with beauty…no ashes."

At home, I put on my tiara and stared in the mirror. No longer focused on the tired face or the swollen-from-crying eyes, I stared only at the tiara. Somehow, I stood straighter…felt stronger. Throughout that day, I wore the tiara while I fixed supper for my son, washed a load of laundry, and cleaned out the toilets. Something about wearing a tiara made even bathroom duty enjoyable. Every time I peeked in the mirror, my tiara reminded me that I was one of God's princesses, the bride of Christ, and my ashes would be transformed into a beautiful crown.

That night I read the entire Isaiah 61 passage and reminded myself that God crowns me with love and mercy, that His love is never manipulative or abusive, and I can depend on His power to change my ashes into beauty. I never have to struggle with the slap of rejection or allow any type of abuse to step over my personal boundaries. Instead, I can smile at myself in the mirror and once again remember how it feels to be the bride of Christ, royalty in the kingdom of God.

Even today, years later, I still wear my tiara. When life hands me a slice of worry and discouragement knocks at my heart, I plant my tiara firmly on my head. Those sparkly rhinestones help me remember my true identity and the reason I was created in the first place: to fulfill God's kingdom plan and live close to His loving heart.

For the woman who feels rejected, it is important to fight against that lie by reminding yourself who you are in Christ. Look in the mirror and tell yourself you are loved and crowned by the King of Kings. He is the One who gives us our true identities.

— RJThesman

❦❦❦❦❦

"To all who mourn in Israel, he will give a crown of beauty for ashes, a joyous blessing instead of mourning, festive praise instead of despair. In their righteousness, they will be like great oaks that the LORD has planted for his own glory." — Isaiah 61:3

❦❦❦❦❦

Prayer

Jesus, we thank You for treating us with respect and value. You are the Prince we long for and the only One who can make us whole. We are grateful to be part of Your royal family, crowned with Your beauty, and living in the aura of Your love. Amen.

Under the Bed

*"The LORD is like a father to his children, tender
and compassionate to those who fear him." — Psalm 103:13*

Most parents dote on their baby's every first. The first tooth, the first few steps, the first words — each one is celebrated.

But not everyone is that blessed. I was one of those little girls who was never sung a lullaby or rocked to sleep at night. My mother didn't wrap her arms around me and whisper how much she loved me. When I fell and skinned my knee, she didn't kiss my booboo and say everything would be okay. Instead, she got angry when I needed glasses because she wouldn't be able to buy herself new shoes.

It didn't take much to aggravate my mother. Dusting my dresser the wrong way could send her into a rage. So it should come as no surprise that at a very early age I figured out my bed was a safe haven when I was frightened.

I would silently crawl underneath the mattresses, scooting to the middle as fast as I could. My mother jabbed me with a broom handle to try to get me to crawl out, but I would wrap my fingers around the wood slats under the box springs and grip with all my might. I didn't realize it only infuriated her more.

I soon discovered I wasn't alone under my bed. It wasn't

an earthly body with me, but I could feel a presence. It didn't scare me; in fact it made me feel secure, wanted, and loved. I now realize it was my heavenly Father.

I felt His strength help me hold on to those wood slats. He wrapped His protective arms around me to keep me warm. He stayed with me time after time under that bed, telling me things I recognize now when I read the Bible.

He told me I would be sheltered and secure. His presence replaced bitterness from the depths of my soul with the sweetness of His love. I learned I needed to let go of the animosity in my heart against those who hurt me. Otherwise, I could cause the same pain in others that I suffered from my mother's hands. I wouldn't heal if I held on to it.

Jesus died on the cross for her transgressions and mine; I needed to forgive my mother to have my sins forgiven. God taught me not to question or judge her, but to trust Him; and He loved and nurtured me when my earthly parents were incapable.

Many of us feel unlovable at times in our lives whether you're five or fifty-five. We have different scars, some visible, most not. But I have learned when you ask, God will heal your scars. I believe He sees them all the same, no matter the source. It doesn't matter to Him; He doesn't question who He heals.

God is present waiting for our acceptance of His love. No matter where you are, what you are doing, how old you are, it's never too late to ask Him to forgive your sins as you forgive others. Ask for His healing so He can give you the same hope He gave me.

- Karen Maag

~~~~~~

"Even if my father and mother abandon me, the Lord will hold me close." — Psalms 27:10

~~~~~~

Prayer

Father, help me today to forgive those who have hurt me. Show me how to let go of the bitterness that has crept into my heart and to see them as You see them — Your child. Reveal Your love to me today and heal these scars, I pray. Amen

A Father's Love

"For his unfailing love toward those who fear him is as great as the height of the heavens above the earth." — **Psalm 103:11**

One summer evening, I was feeling unloved. I knew it wasn't true, but the enemy's lies were so enticing.

Instead of dwelling on my misery, I headed outside to get some fresh air. It was a beautiful, clear night and the sky was ablaze. I couldn't help but think of the words of David, "When I look at the night sky and see the work of your fingers — the moon and the stars you set in place — what are mere mortals that you should think about them, human beings that you should care for them?" (Ps. 8:3–4)

Looking into the heavens, I felt small and alone.

And then I heard His still, small voice.

"How far can you see?"

Looking into that sky it seemed as if I could see forever. Light from stars millions and even billions of light years away twinkled in the sky. And then it dawned on me — light travels at 186,000 miles per second. The distance light travels in one year alone is incredible.

To say that the universe is large is an understatement. There's no way we can comprehend God's creation, and if we can't fully grasp creation, then we can't even begin to fathom God and His ways. As the prophet Isaiah declares, "'My thoughts are nothing like your thoughts,' says the LORD. 'And my ways are far beyond anything you can imagine. For just as the heavens are higher than the earth, so my ways are higher than your ways and my thoughts higher than your thoughts." (Isa. 55:8–9)

Then another verse of Scripture came to mind: "For his unfailing love toward those who fear him is as great as the height of the heavens above the earth." (Ps. 103:11)

Wow! God, who certainly understands the size and scope of the universe, compares it to His love for His children. In the same way I can't comprehend the universe, the thoughts, and the ways of God, I can't fully understand or appreciate God's love for me. In the light of my human limitation what can I do?

Just experience it.

The apostle Paul writes, "For we know how dearly God loves us, because he has given us the Holy Spirit to fill our hearts with his love." (Rom. 5:5)

In light of such glorious revelation how can I not feel loved?

– Ronald D. Johnson

⋙⋙⋙

"When I look at the night sky and see the work of your fingers — the moon and the stars you set in place — what are mere mortals that you should think about them, human beings that you should care for them?" — Psalm 8:3-4

Prayer

Heavenly Father, shine the light of Your love upon me so that I may more completely comprehend Your love. May I allow Your love to shine through me and touch those around me. Amen.

The Precious Gift

"The wind blows, and we are gone — as though we had never been here. But the love of the LORD remains forever with those who fear him." — Psalm 103:16–17

I sat on the bed in my mother's nursing home room as the hospice nurse checked her vital signs. I knew she wouldn't live much longer. A pale, frail woman was all that remained of the proud woman I remembered. God would call her home soon.

My mother worked hard all of her life. Beautiful figurines and crystal sat on the shelves in her china cabinet. Her closets were full of well-tailored clothes and matching shoes. She loved things of material value, but her heart was empty. I teared up thinking of how worthless all her things were to her as she lay in that bed.

I lost track of all the nights she balanced books on my head making me walk back and forth across the living room floor. Etiquette, poise, and confidence were the foundation of her existence.

She also gave of herself to friends. Long after my grandma passed away, she'd visit Grandma's neighbors every Friday morning after her standing hair appointment to write checks for them to pay their bills. She would share excess harvest from her garden with the neighbors. She'd stop whatever she was in the middle of doing to take a call from a friend needing a shoulder to cry on.

Unfortunately, the compassion and helpful nature was shallow. She often complained afterwards her friends were weak and unable to make decisions for themselves.

She never shared her compassion with me. I was willing to accept whatever attention I could get, positive or negative. I just wanted someone to hug and love me, but she just couldn't do it. I've wondered if there ever was a time she wanted a loving, caring relationship with me, but just didn't know how to make it happen.

One particular instance stands out in my mind. I took my mother to her Friday morning beauty shop appointment. As my mother slipped under the dryer, her stylist, Janis pulled me aside.

"Who are you?" she asked. "You act like Virginia's daughter, but I didn't know she had one."

I was shocked! How could a stylist who had worked on my mother's hair for nearly two decades not know she had a daughter, much less grandchildren and a great-grandchild? She knew everything else about both of my parents except what tends to be the first thing most women speak of — their children.

I endured her physical abuse as a child, now this emotional abuse destroyed yet another one of my hopes. I always wanted a mother I could call and ask a question or look to for encouragement when my own kids gave me fits. There was just too much brokenness between us to even suggest such a bold relationship.

Thankfully, I have a heavenly Father whose love for me is unconditional. He's counted every star in heaven and numbered every hair on my head. And He weaves healing within the fibers of my heart by mending my brokenness and healing my wounds.

That confidence gave me comfort and allowed me to pray for my mother that evening in her nursing home room.

It was a precious gift. Because of His love, I was able to share it with my mother on her deathbed in the form of three words. "I forgive you."

– Karen Maag

✥✥✥✥✥

"And the very hairs on your head are all numbered. So don't be afraid; you are more valuable to God than a whole flock of sparrows." — Luke 12:7

✥✥✥✥✥

Prayer

Dear Father, as You count every star and number the hairs on our head, I ask for Your healing graces for the brokenness in each of us. Open our hearts to know Your tenderness through the unconditional love that is ours through the blood of Your Son, Jesus Christ. Teach us to forgive as You have forgiven us. Amen.

Redemption

"He redeems me from death and crowns me
with love and tender mercies." — Psalm 103:4

By the Grace of God

"He redeems me from death..." — Psalm 103:4a

To say I was raised in a dysfunctional family is an understatement. My mom committed suicide when I was sixteen, never once saying, "I love you." I also experienced physical, sexual, and verbal abuse by my father.

Based on what my parents modeled, my idea of love was distorted. I never knew real love, instead self-hatred took up residence in my heart. I believed I was not good enough and needed to work extra hard and give more than others to be loved.

After a divorce, the death of my second husband, and many broken dreams, my heart was crushed and seemed beyond repair. The pain was just too much.

"Just strike me dead," I pleaded with God. I didn't want to kill myself. I vowed to never waste my life the way my mother did. I just didn't want to live.

"So, Coleen, how did you deal with the sexual abuse by your father?" my counselor asked.

"By the grace of God."

"Well, we might want to take a look at that because it would affect any relationship you have with a man."

That statement got me thinking. What did God want from me? Then Psalm 23 came to my mind. "He makes me to lie down in green pastures; He leads me beside the still waters. He restores my soul." (Ps. 23:2–3a NKJV)

The storm clouds of doubt parted and the truth of God's love broke through. God wanted me to rest and trust. I had nothing left in me to give. Like a small child being told to go take a nap, God was asking me to rest in the green, lush pasture of His Word, His care, His loving arms. His number one desire was to restore my soul, that I would know my true worth and value.

The enemy tried to take that value from me. "The thief's purpose is to steal and kill and destroy. My purpose is to give them a rich and satisfying life." (John 10:10) Satan is set out to destroy us, to kill our dreams and steal our self-worth. He's the father of all lies.

Jesus came to redeem us, to tell us the truth about who we are in Him. God who is love, offered Him as a gift. We need only receive it. We can't earn the gift by extra hard work or pay for it by giving until we have nothing left.

Similar to a comprehensive benefit package from an employer, Jesus offers a full benefits package. It's complete, nothing missing, nothing broken.

God took me out of my comfort zone, allowing a painful separation from everyone and everything I'd known, in order to see more clearly.

"'For I know the plans I have for you,' says the LORD. 'They are plans for good and not for disaster, to give you a future and a hope." (Jer. 29:11) I'd been drawn to this verse for years. Now I knew why. God's plan for me was good and was not to harm me.

My life has been redeemed from destruction!

– Coleen Johnson

❦❦❦❦❦

"He makes me to lie down in green pastures; He leads me beside the still waters. He restores my soul." — Psalm 23:2-3a (NKJV)

❦❦❦❦❦

Prayer

Father, I pray today for the imprisoned, the abused, the addicted, the downtrodden — anyone who does not know their true worth and value in You. Please reveal Your love for them today and show them just how valuable they are to You. Amen.

Healing Bad Habits

"He redeems me from death and crowns me
with love and tender mercies." — Psalm 103:4

The foal's ears pricked forward, his black eyes looking me over, as I did him. He was five hours old, and like a newborn child, he needed nourishment from his mother to survive.

No matter how carefully the little guy approached his mother's hindquarters, as soon as he tried to nurse, her thousand-pound body hurtled a hind foot to strike the wall or air. Though my mare, Chassie, lovingly nuzzled her newborn, kicking out whenever something or someone touched her back legs, kept her from giving her foal nourishment.

Chassie pricked her ears forward, looking at me as I entered her stall. She wanted to include me in her joy. She doesn't even realize she's starving him to death, I thought.

Our veterinarian tried everything he could think of, but in the end, left a powder supplement for me to mix with water and feed the foal. Still, he urged me not to give up. The vitamins and minerals in colostrum were vital.

"It is still important to have Chassie nurse her foal," he said. "He needs the bonding experience or he will never grow up to be a normal horse."

I watched Chassie stand over her sleeping offspring, touching him now and then to make sure he was safe. A bond between them had started — she loved him, there was no doubt about it. My heart ached as I sent up a prayer begging God for mercy and help in getting rid of Chassie's bad habit.

Even as we worked with her, still she kicked out. Finally, as my son held the twitch and my husband grabbed a foreleg, she finally stopped kicking. I extracted the colostrum and put it in a glass pop bottle with a lamb's nipple on the end.

The foal drank it down hungrily, sucking down every drop. Two hours later, we tried again. I pushed the colt toward his mother, but he just looked back at me, as if to say, "You first."

As I stretched out my arm, Chassie kicked, finishing off a 2 x 6 inch board. The situation looked hopeless. And as usual, when faced with a circumstance beyond my human endurance, I cried out, "Why, God? Why aren't you helping me?"

I was quickly engulfed by the mists of doubt. Doubt that God could help me. If I didn't get the colt to nurse within twenty-four hours, then, most likely, it wouldn't. There was just a small, tiny pinpoint of light, shining through the dark and bleak future for this foal to have a normal, happy life.

Then one of my friends, a breeder who had experienced this problem before offered her help. She explained the only way to let Chassie know the error of her ways was through discipline. She had to be forced to let go of her bad habit so she could accept and give love.

Finally, harnessed and unable to kick out, Chassie's habit was broken when she felt the tiny lips of her newborn sucking her fears away.

God often does the same with us. Like Chassie, we hate to be told that something we have enjoyed throughout the years is wrong and needs to be abandoned. But those things can become lethal to someone else's welfare.

What issues are you holding onto that can, like a thousand-pound anvil, whisk the happiness from you with one swift kick? Hand it over to your heavenly Father. Through the pain of even our worst circumstances, our merciful God will bring His healing love.

– Catherine Ulrich Brakefield

✦

"For the Son of Man came to seek and save those who are lost." — Luke 19:10

✦

Prayer

Father, reveal those issues in my life that are causing me and others pain. Flood my life with Your grace and mercy, and help me to change these things in my life so I can live a life honoring You. Amen.

What the Locust Have Eaten

"He redeems me from death and crowns me with
love and tender mercies." — Psalm 103:4

At fifty-one, little about my life had turned out the way I planned. My first husband abandoned our two children after learning I was to remarry. My second husband sexually abused my daughter, stealing her innocence and her childhood. That same crime robbed my son of knowing his father and kept me from realizing my dreams of a happy married life.

So much else was lost, including a degree of my faith. "God, restore what the locust have eaten," I prayed one morning. But how could God possibly restore any of this?

For the next several days I watched for answers, but saw none. Before long, caught up in day-to-day stuff, I forgot about my plea.

⁓

"Mom, do you know this person," my twenty-five-year-old daughter Sarah asked as she pointed to a web page. A sense of urgency and excitement filled her voice.

"Your dad's brother had a daughter by that name. Why?"

"I think it's about us."

I read the post. The woman was looking for her two cousins, Matthew and Sarah. She named their parents and that they had both been in the Marines. "Wow, that's us all right," I said. There were too many similarities to ignore.

Sarah mentioned more than once a desire to find her biological father. I had not had so much as a phone call or letter from him in twenty-two years. Sarah was barely four when I remarried, so she had no memories of her father. For her brother it was different. He remembered a dad he loved deeply, but who had disappointed him repeatedly.

I read the post several more times, just to make sure of the facts. All that was left to do was respond. We dashed off an email to the address listed.

"The post is several years old, Sarah, and the email address may not be any good anymore. Don't get your hopes too high," I admonished. Then she and my five-year-old grandson went home to wait.

They didn't have to wait long. The email bounced back undeliverable. Maybe I had typed the address wrong or read it incorrectly? Maybe those *ones* were actually *L*s. I sent the email again, this time with a different address, but it was no use. The address was too old.

I called Sarah. I sensed her disappointment in the deep sigh I heard through the phone.

"Is there some other way we could contact her?"

"I've already searched for a address or a phone number, but I haven't found one. I'll keep trying, but I can't make any promises."

I spent the rest of the evening searching. I found too many too many people with the same name. I finally took an educated guess based on geographic location, wrote a letter, and snail mailed it. I prayed and went to bed.

Barely a week passed when I received an email in answer to my letter. I called Sarah and told her. Miraculously, the letter had found its way to the right woman. The email explained that Sarah's dad had searched for us for several years, but without success. He had given up; she hadn't.

After twenty-two years and a few strategic phone calls, Sarah, her brother, and their dad were about to be reunited.

During my prayer time a few days later, the Lord reminded me of my request to restore what the locust had taken. A month had passed since I'd sent that doubtful prayer on its way to heaven. James 1:6 says "But when you ask him, be sure that your faith is in God alone. Do not waver, for a person with divided loyalty is as unsettled as a wave of the sea that is blown and tossed by the wind."

God knew my weakness, but saw my heart. Despite my doubt, with tender mercies and compassion, He answered.

– Debra L. Butterfield

"But when you ask him, be sure that your faith is in God alone. Do not waver, for a person with divided loyalty is as unsettled as a wave of the sea that is blown and tossed by the wind." — James 1:6

Prayer

Father, thank You for all You have done for me. I admit, sometimes in my busyness I often miss Your answers to my prayers. Please bring back to my memory all of the good things You have done for me and reveal the answers I have missed. Amen.

The Prodigal Daughter

*"He redeems me from death and crowns me
with love and tender mercies." — Psalm 103:4*

When I moved to Oceanside, California, with my Marine husband in the late 1980s, I thought it would be the answer to all of our problems in our troubled marriage. It wasn't. Things got worse. Eventually, I walked away from what little faith I had left from childhood. My family was heartbroken over my choices and the vows to my husband were shattered like glass by infidelity on both sides.

I knew more about the bars than the churches in Oceanside. I could point out places of ill repute and apartments where nightly parties continued until dawn.

After my divorce I tried to get my act together, but I was just too far gone. I didn't think God could ever love me. Visiting churches left me with hot guilt in the pit of my stomach that only fueled the downward spiral I called my life.

People in Oceanside knew me. They knew me as the fun loving party girl on the arm of a different Marine every weekend. They knew me as a liar and a thief who did what she had to do to get by. They knew me for every wicked manipulation I used in an attempt to make everything okay.

Before I left the city I tried to clean up. I tried to do honorable things. I tried to make up to my parents for all of the pain I caused them. But I couldn't do it. I couldn't be good enough.

Eventually, I met and married another Marine. The day we wed we both knew we didn't love each other, and neither of us was interested in serving a God whom we'd long forgotten. Still, I thought it was the honorable thing to do.

The day he finished his service in the Corps, we headed to my husband's home in the middle of the Midwest.

I was thrilled. No one knew me there. I could become honorable. I could change who I was. I didn't have to be the woman Oceanside created anymore.

It was in Missouri that I realized I needed a redeemer. Nothing I did could change anything about my past. It haunted every memory. I needed someone who could take the mess I made of my life and make something better from it. That someone was Jesus.

My life was truly different in Christ. Serving God was everything to me. He healed my heart and a marriage that should have never made it past the honeymoon. I trusted completely in the Lord, and I never looked back to my life in Oceanside.

~~~~~

Seventeen years later, I faced an invitation to participate in a retreat at a monastery overlooking the Pacific, in Oceanside. As a Christian writer and speaker, I wasn't sure I wanted to go back to the place where my demons dined. I knew I was a new creation in Christ. I knew my sins were cast as far as the east is from the west. I knew there was nothing in Oceanside that could harm me. But the thought of all I had done in that city brought tears to my eyes. I decided to go, if for no other reason than to prove my past could not control my future.

One of the retreat's disciplines involved silent prayer and meditation on the Word of God. As we set out on a three-hour adventure, completely alone in the quiet of the gardens on the hillside, all I could think of was how bored I would be. I found a wooden bench near an olive tree. It faced the Pacific Ocean, so at least the view was pretty.

I breathed the ocean breeze deep into my lungs. I missed it more than I realized. "Okay God, you brought me here, now what?" I whispered, almost guilty for breaking the silence.

The breeze picked up, blowing a red rose from out of nowhere to my feet. I reached for it as tears fell, splashing the flower with droplets that looked like dew. Scripture filled my mind as the Spirit of God embraced my heart.

"Look, the winter is past, and the rains are over and gone. The flowers are springing up, the season of singing birds has come, and the cooing of turtledoves fills the air. The fig trees are forming young fruit, and the fragrant grapevines are blossoming. Rise up, my darling! Come away with me, my fair one!" (Song 2:11–13)

Suddenly everything made sense. It was easy for me to walk and talk like a changed person in the Midwest. But I didn't know the truth of Christ's redemption until I understood He called me out of the winter of my youth, and into His plan for my life.

During my days as a prodigal in Oceanside, my heart searched for love, but never truly found it. God had to take me back to the place of my transgression to show me, even there, He loved me.

I will never look at Oceanside as a place of sorrow and sin again. God has redeemed me; He has redeemed the place of my trouble and He has called to me, "Rise up, my darling, come away."

– Pamela Sonnenmoser

❦❦❦❦

"O Israel, hope in the LORD; for with the LORD there is unfailing love. His redemption overflows." — Psalm 130:7

❦❦❦❦

Prayer

Heavenly Father, thank You for redeeming me from my past and giving me a new future. Please show to me today just how much You love me. Help me to remember that Your Son's sacrifice was all that was needed for me to put my past behind me. Please show me how to leave it there, Lord. Amen.

Healing

"..and heals all my diseases." — *Psalm 103:3b*

Youth Not Wasted

*"He fills my life with good things. My youth is
renewed like the eagle's!" — Psalm 103:5*

It was odd for me to be turning forty — I mean, that's not just an age, it's a new decade!

I have a specific memory of looking at my parents during my senior year and thinking how old that number was. Yes, I used the word *old*. We were a family of three teenage girls, with both parents working full-time. Then they added a fourth child to our family that year.

Of course, they seemed old. They were so tired they couldn't see straight! I promised myself I wouldn't be like that when I was their age. I would be a hip, non-married, career woman, who always had it together. Without going into twenty years of details, let's just say God had different plans for me.

So, as I counted down each month of year thirty-nine, I was faced with how I would accept this new chapter of my life. I surely wasn't going to enter my forties the same way my parents did.

We didn't have teenagers or one on the way. I was a stay-at-home mom just sending my kiddos off to elementary school. Could I do it with grace and poise? Did I have to say that number and think at the same time, man that's old?

I admit, for the last ten years, I felt ancient. My thirties were spent with no make-up, ponytails, sweats, little to no sleep, and just a basic feeling of misery.

I was tired of being tired, grumpy, and ungrateful for the life the Lord had blessed me with. After all, hadn't I prayed for the very children I now complained were stealing my youth? Me, a mother of three, who had been told I would never have kids. Me, a wife of nearly eighteen years, in the age of rising divorce rates. Me, a child of God, who has a life filled with more good things than I deserve.

"You have turned my mourning into joyful dancing. You have taken away my clothes of mourning and clothed me with joy, that I might sing praises to you and not be silent. O LORD my God, I will give you thanks forever!" (Ps. 30:11–12)

The verse was my gift and it armed me with a new attitude. I read it in a Bible study one day and it jumped off the page. I didn't have to face any of this alone. He clothes me with joy and puts the song in my heart. I knew with the Lord's help, I could face the new chapter of my life with a new outlook and confidence. I made the choice to give thanks, dance, and not be silent.

I am now in my forties and feel wonderful. I do feel my youth renewed — not physically because quite honestly, I'm still tired 99 percent of the time. Instead, He renewed my youth by blessing me with a young heart, a new love for Him and blessings I didn't even know were possible.

It is a daily choice, no matter what path we're facing. Are you considering what college you should attend? Do you have a terminally ill child in desperate need of a parent's positive attitude? Are you wiping spit-up off your clothes for the fiftieth time this week? Are you facing a new chapter of life, whether it be a new decade or an empty nest?

I encourage you to focus on the good things. If you can't see past the struggles right now, start with one. Rest in the promise that He will renew you every day to face these new challenges with a great spirit. Have confidence in your blessings and before long, you'll have to search for the challenges.

- Alycia Holston

~ttttt~

"You have turned my mourning into joyful dancing. You have taken away my clothes of mourning and clothed me with joy, that I might sing praises to you and not be silent. O Lord my God, I will give you thanks forever!" — Psalm 30:11–12

~ttttt~

Prayer

Heavenly Father, thank You for all the good things You place in our lives. Help us to turn our eyes toward Your abundant blessings. Help us to face our new chapters with grace and confidence. We give You thanks forever and ever! Amen.

Full Circle

"His salvation extends to the children's children
of those who are faithful to his covenant, of those
who obey his commandments!" — Psalm 103:17b-18

The screaming and crying were doable. The hives were almost doable. But at midnight, I was still holding her.

As I sang "Jesus Loves Me," "The Itsy Bitsy Spider," and "You are my Sunshine," and rocked her, I felt her little muscles relax and watched as her long eyelashes drooped.

She has perfect features, I thought. What a beautiful princess.

But as I laid her down in the crib, her muscles tensed, the hives returned, and the sobbing was back.

By three a.m. she finally cried herself to sleep in the crib with a death grip on my finger through the slats. Her brother slept nearby, having snoozed through the whole thing.

Finally, it was my turn. Tears ran down my cheeks as I quietly sobbed. Careful not to disturb her, I sat there with my arm still attached to this little wonder and thought about how God chose to put her under our roof.

The next morning both kids were up early. Sleep deprived and jonesing for caffeine, we made it to our doctor's appointment and our meeting with all of the invested children's division officials. We ate lunch and found nap time not nearly as traumatic.

Was it the light? Did she know it will only be a short while?

But that night was back to the same thing and after three nights in a row, I started to question what we had gotten ourselves into. Was it really what we wanted to do?

As I thought about it, I realized the answer was no. It was not what I wanted, but what God wanted for me. It was what He needed for me. It is what He needed for them and for our family.

Not only that, but it is so much more. I soon discovered it was how He would bless me more than He could by growing our family in a traditional way. Just as Esther was called for such a time like this, God called us for this.

Our placement took place during my winter vacation as a teacher. I did not have to take time off to get them to all of their doctor appointments, get haircuts or go shopping for clothing, diapers and anything else we needed. My husband's work was slow. He was home to help me out as our family transitioned to having two more kids in our home.

And while Christmas doesn't appear to be the best time to take a child away from their biological family, we were blessed with the celebration of adding safety, consistency, security, and love to their lives. Something they had never known before.

While my children got a second chance, they have given me more than I can ever give back to them.

What does God want to use in your life to bring you full circle? In Romans, Paul wrote, "Oh, how great are God's riches and wisdom and knowledge! How impossible it is for us to understand his decisions and his ways! For who can know the LORD's thoughts? Who knows enough to give him advice? And who has given him so much that he needs to pay it back? For everything comes from him and exists by his power and is intended for his glory. All glory to him forever! Amen." (Rom. 11:33–36)

God knew what He was doing. When I developed endometriosis, He had a plan to fulfill my desire for children. He knew what He was doing every time I was disappointed and had not conceived. He knew what He was doing every time we felt like we could not help our two. He knew what He was doing when He allowed the children to go through what they went through. He sustained them. He allowed them to be nourished.

We have come full circle. He knows for your situation, dear friend. Let Him bring you full circle, too.

- Crystal Nichols

⟊⟊⟊⟊⟊

"Oh, how great are God's riches and wisdom and knowledge! How impossible it is for us to understand his decisions and his ways! For who can know the LORD's thoughts? Who knows enough to give him advice? And who has given him so much that he needs to pay it back? For everything comes from him and exists by his power and is intended for his glory. All glory to him forever! Amen." — Romans 11:33-36

⟊⟊⟊⟊⟊

Prayer

Today, Father will be a day that marks a new road of healing, a point on a circle that will change our knowledge of who You are. Help us to recognize our benefits in You. Your compassion and healing in our lives is evident every day and we receive that today. Help our unseeing eyes to be open. Amen.

A Weekend in ICU

"...and heals all my diseases." — Psalm 103:3b

God is still in the healing business. In America, miraculous healings seem rare and unusual. But in foreign, often third world countries, miraculous healings occur regularly. Why, then, with all the promises of God's healing mercies contained within Scripture, does it seem so few healings occur within our American churches? Could it be that Americans are so blessed with advanced medical services and clinics, we are more inclined to put our faith in our doctor instead of the God who is Jehovah-Rapha, God our Healer!

Despite this lack of faith, God still performs miracles. We just need to know where to look and how to recognize the healings amongst us. The best place to look for it is where there is no other hope or option. Desperation has a way of turning us to God as our only hope!

In 2003, I was that desperate. Shortly after my second son was born, I contracted a severe blood infection that nearly killed me. What I initially thought was the flu turned deadly. I was rushed to the nearest VA hospital in Shreveport, Louisiana. It was a two-hour trip, and on the way my vitals began to fade. My wife was convinced she would lose me.

I was admitted to the hospital that Friday afternoon severely dehydrated — my internal organs in danger of shutting down. The blood infection was so serious, doctors said it would kill me before the antibiotics could take effect. The only option was a blood transfusion.

The hospital was out of my rare blood type so they began a desperate search of nearby hospitals and blood banks. Meanwhile, they hooked me up to five saline IV drips to rehydrate me and keep my kidneys and other organs from shutting down.

My life literally hung in the balance. With one foot in the grave, I was fading fast. In the waiting room, far from family, friends, church members, or a pastor, my wife huddled with my two small boys and cried out for God to intervene.

As minutes turned into hours, nurses checked my thready pulse and fluids to see if I was improving, or at least, hanging on. They drew my blood every hour, to see if I was responding to the antibiotic that was trying to hold off the infection until some blood could be found.

The weekend arrived and compounded the struggle to find the blood I so desperately needed. Unable to eat, barely conscious, and still severely dehydrated despite the continuous IV feeds, I knew I might not make it.

My wife returned home and called everyone she could, asking them to pray for me. I was alone in that hospital room. There was no one I could reach out to except God. So I did.

Like David said in Psalm 30:8–9, "I cried out to you, O Lord. I begged the Lord for mercy, saying, 'What will you gain if I die, if I sink into the grave? Can my dust praise you? Can it tell of your faithfulness?'" I knew I was dying. I knew when I did, my death would leave my wife to raise our children alone. I knew my boys would grow up without their daddy, and my parents would outlive their youngest son. But I also knew God and I cried out to him from a place of lonely, hopeless desperation. And I know He heard my prayer.

Three days without hope. Three days without healing. But Sunday held the promise.

It's fitting that on the Lord's Day I felt God come into that hospital room. I knew the moment I was healed. When the nurse came in at the top of the hour to draw blood, I managed a weak smile and a witty comment about the staff being only interested in my blood and not my brains. It was the first time I'd been able to speak, much less be coherent in days. From that moment on I grew stronger and by that night I ate my first real meal.

By Monday morning I could sit up on the edge of the bed and walk to the bathroom. When the doctors came in later that morning, I expected them to tell me they'd found the blood I was so desperate for. Instead, they said the words I was sure I wouldn't hear. "Your blood work over the weekend came back completely normal. You're getting discharged."

From a place of complete and utter desperation I experienced the miraculous. God intervened on my behalf. Coincidence could not explain how I went from death's door to completely recovered in four days. But I know the answer. It was God. He still "heals all my diseases."

- Wendon Pettey

⸙⸙⸙⸙⸙

"I cried out to you, O LORD. I begged the Lord for mercy, saying, 'What will you gain if I die, if I sink into the grave? Can my dust praise you? Can it tell of your faithfulness?'" — Psalm 30:8–9

Prayer

O God, when it seems all avenues are exhausted and all hope has failed in my hour of need, I turn to You. You alone are able to heal the disease that afflicts me night and day! Only You can speak the words that restore life and rebuke the death that even now sits at my door! You are the God that heals all my sicknesses, and I cry out to You in desperation for a touch from Your mighty hand. My hope, my future, my everything lie in Your hand of mercy and grace. Extend it to me, I pray, and restore my flesh…my spirit… my mind. Quicken me once again by Your mighty Spirit and make me whole. Touch me, Lord, and heal me. Amen.

A Life to the Fullest

"The L<small>ORD</small> has made the heavens his throne;
from there he rules over everything." — Psalm 103:19

L
eon gripped the wheel. "Tell me again. What happened?" My husband kept his eyes fixed on the road.

"Some guys robbed a bank in Lincoln. They led the police on a high-speed chase toward Omaha." I repeated what our sister-in-law told me. "Somewhere along the way they drove off the interstate, cut across a cornfield, and ended up at your sister's place. In the midst of stealing the truck, they shot Retha and Les."

"They're both alive, right?" I felt the car accelerate.

"Yes," I assured him, "but Les was shot in the head."

Silence. I prayed as I watched the highway lines zip past. I couldn't remember a time our family rode in such stillness.

When we arrived at the hospital four hours later, more than fifty of Retha and Les's relatives filled the emergency room. Their daughter, Hope, met us with a hug and a dazed look, while Brandon, her brother, paced like a caged tiger.

Leon weaved his way through the sea of familiar, but somber faces toward his elderly father. His siblings stood guard near their dad.

"The doctors just told us they'll both go into surgery soon, but we can go in to see them first." One of Leon's brothers updated us. "We're trying to keep Brandon calm; he wants to go see the house. Hope is doing pretty well, considering…"

"Where were they shot? What are the injuries?" Leon asked.

"Retha took five shots. They hit her bladder, kidney, and spleen." His brother ran a hand across his abdomen. "Les was shot in the head and the stomach. The doctor said an inch to the right, the bullet might have missed him; an inch to the left, it would have killed him."

Did I hear him right? This doesn't happen to people we know…to our family!

A nurse led the immediate families to see their loved ones, and then over the next few hours, I continued my silent prayers. Brothers and sisters paced. Parents clutched tissues. Nephews and nieces found places to lie on the thinly carpeted floors to sleep. Others curled up in the hard plastic chairs. I heard sniffles and chuckles as a few shared stories. Dings and dongs summoned hospital staff.

An eerie silence fell on the room when the doctor sat down with Hope, Brandon, and Leon's dad. The rest of us crowded around. "We removed her spleen along with eighteen inches of intestine. We had to cut away a small portion of a kidney and the bladder has two holes to heal."

As I listened, I envisioned God's angels swishing to and fro keeping the 9mm bullets from killing them — either of them. They're both alive.

The doctor scanned the crowd. "Do you have any other questions?"

"How's Les?" His father asked. A tear glistened on the old iron worker's face.

"He's still in surgery." The doctor rose to leave. "Someone should be in to update you soon."

An hour or so passed before his doctor came. Once again

we gathered around. "We opened his frontal lobe to remove the bullet and clean the gun residue from the sinus cavity. We couldn't save the eye. After the socket heals, he'll be fitted for a glass eye. The next twenty-four hours are crucial, but he's out of danger." The doctor left and the family exhaled.

Over the next few days, we heard of the shooters' arrest and doctors gave us positive medical reports. Family members readied the house for Retha and Les's homecoming by replacing the bullet-ridden door and cleaning up blood stains from the floor, walls, and furnishings.

"How will You wash away the memories?" I asked the Lord as I packed for home. "Thank You for sparing their lives. Lay Your mighty hand upon them and bring healing to their bodies, minds, and spirits."

Leon, the boys, and I stopped at the hospital one last time before leaving Lincoln. A critical care nurse escorted us to the room they now shared. Les, wearing a patch over his eye socket, squirted our boys with a water-filled syringe. Retha giggled. "I'm sorry."

Our visit was short, but Retha shared their resolve to not let the shooting define them. "We want to go back to our normal lives. We want to go to the grandkids' ball games and dance recitals. We even want to go back to work." Les moaned and squirted the boys with another shot of water.

Leon gave his big sister a gentle hug. "I love you, Sis."

"I love you, little brother." Retha patted him on the back.

Our drive home was filled with songs of praise. We talked of God's mercy. I shared my thoughts of the angels blocking the bullets. Leon mentioned all who witnessed this miracle — believers, nonbelievers, and undecideds. And we prayed.

Lives were changed the day two men tried to steal, kill, and destroy our family. Retha and Les chose to live their new normal life to its fullest. Hope, Brandon, and their children's faith grew stronger. Leon's soft-spoken father acknowledged God's glory more freely. According to a newspaper report, one of the two men who burst into their home said the couple's survival "made him believe in God."

A ripple effect of healing went beyond the bullet wounds. God's love and mercy blocked the spray of anxiety, fear, and hate with peace to live life to its fullness.

– Merrie Hansen

❧❧❧❧❧❧

"The thief's purpose is to steal and kill and destroy. My purpose is to give them a rich and satisfying life." — John 10:10

❧❧❧❧❧❧

Prayer

Heavenly Father, thank You for Your protection and healing mercies. Please be with those hurting today and show them Your grace and mercy. Grant them peace and may their lives be a witness of your healing power. Amen.

Justice

"The LORD gives righteousness and justice to all who are treated unfairly." — Psalm 103:6

The Bully

*"The LORD gives righteousness and justice
to all who are treated unfairly." — Psalm 103:6*

I was a very shy thirteen-year-old girl as I made my way to school the first day of eighth grade. And I was scared to death.

Normally, I would walk to school, but since it was the first day, my father drove me. While I was blossoming into a young woman, my mind-set was still that of a little girl. That's why I chose my best party dress to wear that day. I recall it well — black velvet bodice and flowing, pleated, pale-blue chiffon. I felt like a princess.

My world came crashing down, however, when I got my homeroom seat assignment. The school bully, "Raymond" was sitting right behind me. From that moment on, he singled me out as the target of his vicious and cruel remarks. I cringed with every foul name he threw my way.

Day after day he hammered away, spewing hate and insults, occasionally getting others to chime in as he mercilessly made fun of me. The verbal abuse was so severe and embarrassing that I did not report it to teachers, or even to my parents. I simply endured…suffering silently. I'm convinced if I had not come from a loving and secure home-life, the torment would have had a severe and profound effect on me.

After months of abuse, I finally realized it was something I could pray about. So I took my request to the Lord — asking him to stop Raymond's tirades against me.

Less than a week later, a new student came into our homeroom. "John" was older and wore a black leather jacket with a snake embossed across the back. He commanded the respect of the other students. We knew he was only there until he was old enough to quit school, but no one was going to mess with him in the meantime.

His first day, as we lined up for lunch, my nemesis, Raymond, took the opportunity to rail at me with one of his foulmouthed insults.

"Hey, leave Blondie alone," John growled as he poked Raymond in the chest.

That was all it took. The bully never insulted me again.

John didn't stay in school very long. In fact, he and I never interacted as friends. I don't recall that we ever had a conversation, before or after his one comment that brought my deliverance. To me, John was an angel sent from heaven. I'm often reminded of that time in my life and wonder why I waited so long to pray about that situation.

Even now, as a grandmother, there are times I forget the Lord is concerned about every single phase of my life. So many times I endure, when I could take even the most seemingly insignificant problem to Jesus.

Matthew tells us in his gospel the very hairs of our heads are numbered. And the psalmist urges not to forget all of God's benefits (Ps. 103:2).

He is not only our Savior, Healer, Deliverer, Comforter, and much more — He is also a very caring and loving Father, eager and willing to minister to His children.

What a personal God we serve. He cared about that timid,

skinny, thirteen-year-old girl who was the victim of a bully. He cares about each and every situation and circumstance we face.

My heavenly Daddy took care of that bully for me, without threat, without a scene…in a wise and miraculous way. He keeps a close watch, even noting how many hairs are on our head — and He'll send ministering angels, if necessary, to rescue — or He'll give us the grace and strength to endure a difficulty. Oh, the benefits He offers!

— Sharon Spiegel

❦

"What is the price of two sparrows — one copper coin? But not a single sparrow can fall to the ground without your Father knowing it. And the very hairs on your head are all numbered." — Matthew 10:29–30

❦

Prayer

Lord, help me to rely more on You, Your benefits and fatherly care. Remind me to turn to You not only for the big things in my life, but even the seemingly insignificant problems I face. Amen.

A Gift of Grace

"The LORD is...slow to get angry and
filled with unfailing love." — Psalm 103:8b

In the summer of 1966, when I was six years old, my father decided to move our family. He loaded my mom, brother, two sisters, and myself in our car and left Wyoming heading west.

I felt something foreboding as we traveled. I couldn't quite tell what was bothering me. It was simply a sense of dread. It was as if my whole life was about to change and I knew I would never be the same.

"It's getting dark, Daddy. We better turn around and go home," I pleaded.

But we kept traveling, not stopping until we reached a migrant camp on the outskirts of Portland, Oregon. The camp had several cabins, ours was a one-room shack with a dining area on one end and two large bunk beds on the other. Our new home was also the only one with cold running water, which came from a spigot on the outside of the cabin.

The children worked alongside of their families, from sunrise to sunset, picking strawberries to bring in more money. There were no bars, fences, or guns to keep the families working, but there was harsh poverty and a certain stigma. I remember getting called Oakies even though we were from Wyoming.

My second day in the camp, I sat practicing my *ABC*s in the dirt with a stick, when a girl around my age came up, introduced herself, and asked my name.

"Peggy."

The girl studied me intently. "What are you doing?"

"Practicing my *ABC*s."

Her face lit up. "What's that?"

I didn't understand the implications of what she was saying. "You know, the alphabet!"

She drew in a deep, excited breath. "Would you show me?"

Over the next few months I taught the girl the alphabet using a stick in the dirt. It thrilled me to see she was an eager and fast learner.

Missionaries often came to the camp to read, play games, and sing with the children on Sundays; their only day off.

Toward the end of the picking season, the group put on a fair for the children. They set up a booth where each child could pick out one toy. I chose a pack with two dolls and their home-made wardrobe. I grabbed my new toys and started walking away from everyone to inspect them, when one of the missionaries handed me a sack with toothpaste, toothbrush, soap, and a washcloth in it. I was so excited, I ran to show my mom the pack, leaving my new dolls behind.

When I returned a short time later, I found my alphabet friend and her sister playing with my new toys. Outraged, I stomped off to grab my dolls out of their hands.

"Peggy, what's wrong?" one of the missionary women asked.

"Those girls stole my dolls!"

The woman and her friend smiled, as if it were no big deal. "Go and get another one."

I was furious. They were supposed to do something.

"But the Bible says, 'Thou shalt not steal,'" I yelled. My days in Sunday school had taught me about the Ten Commandments, but not much more. I used my limited biblical knowledge to show off. If they weren't going to obey me, they had to obey the Word of God.

The women just smiled at each other. "Jesus also said if someone takes your cloak do not stop him from taking your tunic. And those without love are a clanging cymbal," she said. "We know you don't understand right now but someday you will. Besides, those girls need the dolls more than you do. Go and choose another doll!"

They were right. As I started to walk away one called out to me, "You are going to receive a great gift. You don't have to do anything with it; all we ask is you always remember this place."

I ran off and picked up the very last doll. She had matted hair and lipstick stains, but somehow it didn't seem to matter.

Two weeks later a couple of missionaries came to the camp and told us they had found a home for us in Lake Oswego. My dad would also have a new job at a high school in Portland. Life was about to change, again.

That Christmas I received a brand new doll who I was convinced was the great gift I was to receive. As I look back now, I realize I received so much more than a doll and a new place to live. God gave me the precious gift of grace.

- Peggy Kennedy

"He gives justice to the oppressed and food to the hungry. The LORD frees the prisoners." — Psalm 146:7

Prayer

Lord, thank You for Your justice. May we, Your servants, use our gifts for the benefit of all, for Your glory to reach a hurting world. Amen.

An Important Conversation

The LORD gives righteousness and justice to all
who are treated unfairly." — Psalm 103:6

I don't know. It seems like a waste of money"

"Go. You want to go."

"Are you sure?"

"Yes, go with my blessing."

While I drove the five hours to my parents' house, my husband's words replayed in my head. "Go with my blessing." The reason for the week-long trip was simple…even selfish. I wanted to visit family and friends without any particular agenda.

The morning after I arrived, Mom and Dad's muffled voices woke me. I imagined them in the kitchen. Dad seated in his chair with a cup of coffee and Mom up puttering about.

I heard the two of them leave to run errands, so I got up and took advantage of the quiet surroundings to talk with the Lord. I sat at a wobbly card table engrossed in my Bible study when Dad appeared at the door. "What are you reading?" he asked.

"Oh, it's on revival." I placed a finger on my page.

He pulled out a chair and sat down. "What does the Bible say about grudges?"

"Well, we need to let them go." I slipped a bookmark in my page.

"What about sixty years of anger?"

I slid the book aside. "God give me wisdom," I silently prayed.

"Since my dad died when I was twelve, the high school principal decided I needed a little discipline when I misbehaved," my hero dad explained. Over the next few minutes he revealed the pain he had endured as a child.

"I don't know what I did to deserve such a beating." Dad's sad blue eyes pleaded for answers. My heart broke. I listened, whispering another heartfelt prayer to heaven.

"Your mom doesn't understand why I sometimes wake in the middle of the night angry for no reason," Dad clenched his fists. "It's him. He haunts me."

Growing up, I'd witnessed my father's strange outbursts of rage and saw those same big hands bang on a table without explanation. I still cringe when I think of how he'd slam his fist against the dashboard as he drove down the road mumbling to himself.

"Dad, you need to forgive him. Ask God to help you. Your anger is like a cancer eating away your peace. Forgiveness is the only way to stop it."

I didn't press, but let him absorb the idea of forgiving someone he could no longer confront face to face.

A look of relief slowly replaced the pain on his face. We talked a few minutes longer. When Mom returned home the conversation turned to other topics, but my prayers did not.

Over the next few days, Dad and I cheered for our favorite college football team from the living room couch. My sister and her husband joined us for an evening of card playing, with plenty of laughter and good-hearted razzing. Mom took a snapshot of Dad with an ear-to-ear grin on his face and an arm around his dog… but not another word about grudges or forgiveness was spoken.

Wednesday morning dawned with the smell of harvest in the air. The sun shone bright and warm. Mom and I drove to my aunt's for a visit while Dad left to meet friends for coffee in town.

When Mom and I returned home, I saw the little tractor in the corner of the acreage. "Your dad needs to drain the hydraulic fluid and he uses the hill to let gravity help," she explained as she waved toward the hill and headed to the house.

She sorted the mail on the kitchen table. "I'm going to see how he's doing," she finally said. The screen door banged as she left.

A few minutes later, it slammed again. "I think your dad is dead," she said calmly.

I jumped up from the couch, brushing past her as she dialed 911. I darted out the door and rushed up the hill through the pasture grass to my dad. Tears ran down my cheeks as I looked heavenward. "O God, he forgave that man, didn't he?"

Mom joined me a few moments later as I stood over his motionless body and waited for help to come. She looked at me.

"You're here."

"I know." Go with my blessing echoed in my heart.

When I decided to take this week-long trip, I had no idea it would be to engage in such an important conversation.

To forgive those who sin against us not only relieves them of guilt, but it frees us from the bondage of our anger. Forgiving someone who is no longer in our life or not even alive, can be difficult, but it is necessary to be freed.

My dad never shared all the details of this incident, but I know that while the beating left no physical scars on his body, the humiliation crushed his fatherless-teenage-boy-struggling-to-become-a-man's heart.

After sixty-years, Dad, tired of clinging to the anger, was ready to be set free. As Christ said, "If you forgive those who sin against you, your heavenly Father will forgive you. But if you refuse to forgive others, your Father will not forgive your sins." (Matt. 6:14–15)

I don't know with absolute certainty that my dad forgave

this man, but I believe with all my heart he did…and died a man at peace.

Go with God's blessing, Dad.

– Merrie Hansen

✦✦✦✦✦✦

"If you forgive those who sin against you, your heavenly Father will forgive you. But if you refuse to forgive others, your Father will not forgive your sins." — Matthew 6:14–15

✦✦✦✦✦✦

Prayer

Heavenly Father, I want to have a forgiving spirit. Please show me how to forgive those who have treated me unfairly, and help me to let go of the pain and release the anger. Amen.

Revelation

"He revealed his character to Moses and his deeds to the people of Israel." — Psalm 103:7

Big Girl Bike

"He revealed his character to Moses and his
deeds to the people of Israel." — Psalm 103:7

What an exciting day! We purchased my three-year-old her first bike and she could hardly wait to get it home so that she could try it out on the sidewalk in front of our house. While her father and I knew it might be a bit too big for her, she was determined to ride it.

Decked out in her helmet, we went in the front yard to give it a go. She climbed on and wobbled around a bit without going anywhere. She couldn't quite figure out the pedals. She climbed off and stared at it in silence.

"Would you like Mommy or Daddy to help you ride it for a while?" I offered.

She shook her head. "No, I'm a big girl. I can do it."

A few seconds later she climbed back on. Again, the bike didn't budge.

"I *am* a big girl," she whispered to herself. "I can do it. I can ride a bike. I know how. I'm three."

I smiled as I sat there watching her figure it out. I admired her confidence. So many times, when I'm struggling with life, I pout or look for the easy way out.

Wouldn't God be overjoyed if for once, when things aren't

going well, I reminded myself what a big Christian I am? I have been a believer for almost twenty years. In that time I have faced some tough stuff and not once has God failed me. He always delivers me and provides hope. Instead of acting like a child, wouldn't it be better to walk through life's troubles with a confidence in His faithfulness?

Our lives will always have unexpected twists. When we are tempted to worry and fear, we need to remind ourselves what we know to be true of our God. We have seen His power, we have experienced His deliverance, and our futures are certain. We don't need to worry and doubt. He will give us the strength and diligence to walk through trials reflecting His glory.

- Holly Hauskins

⚜

"But Jesus said, 'Let the children come to me. Don't stop them! For the Kingdom of Heaven belongs to those who are like these children." — Matthew 19:14

⚜

Prayer

Heavenly Father, thank You for Your faithfulness in our lives. We are grateful that You do not abandon us when life gets tough. We pray that when we face trials, we will choose to remember who You are, who You have always been and who You promise Your children can be when trusting in You. Give us the confidence of a child. Let us honor and bring glory to You when walking through difficult times. Amen.

The Word Returns

"Let all that I am praise the LORD; may I never forget the good things he does for me." — Psalm 103:2

My husband was devastated. It only took a moment that Sunday morning to lose something precious to him, but as he soon discovered, it gave God an opportunity to reveal His love for us.

I was serving in an after-church ministry that morning as Mike corralled our kids into the van to take them home. He was concentrating so hard on our precious cargo that he placed his Bible on top of our van and forgot about it. He didn't realize it was gone until he was home.

He was heartbroken. This good friend had been with him through thick and thin for more than a decade. He had invested study, notes, prayer, conversations, and love into the relationship.

We scoured the route to and from church many times that day…ten miles of curves, pavement, and highway traffic with hazards flashing…to no avail. He was convinced it got caught in the luggage rack and rode that way for a while before sailing into a ditch.

We didn't have any better luck after the fourth time and finally handed it over to the Lord. There was a reason the book went for a ride that snowy day. Maybe it was meant for somebody else to find. Still, we were sad. It held some special meaning for my husband.

Praying for the person who found it to be blessed, we loaded up the kiddos one more time and headed to the evening church service.

As we walked in the door, we stopped to talk to a friend who had helped with the search. We were filling him in when the children's group leader passed by. She told us a woman stopped her on the way into church and had returned a Bible. Could it be ours? We rushed over to the table to discover Mike's Bible sitting in a plastic bag.

This woman saw a book on the interstate, pulled over, got out, and picked it up. She thought it was either a school book or Bible, but felt it was important. We could tell it had been run over — a pen and some cough drops inside the cover were pulverized — but the Bible was fine. She was able to return it the same day thanks to the church bulletin tucked inside.

As we drove home that evening, I just could not help but think of the verse in Isaiah, "The grass withers and the flowers fade, but the word of our God stands forever."

- Alycia Holston

❦

"The grass withers and the flowers fade,
but the word of our God stands forever." — Isaiah 40:8

Prayer

Father, we know that You love us and protect us. We are so thankful for the provision in our lives. Thank You for caring for even our material things. We are so grateful for the precious Word You have given us and the book that serves as our guide. We praise You for all the good things You give us. Amen

Finding Ellie

"His salvation extends to the children's children
of those who are faithful to his covenant, of those
who obey his commandments!" — Psalm 103:17b-18

God is in control." I closed my eyes. "He really is in control."

My mantra wasn't working. Sitting in that tiny Ukrainian apartment I was scared — and heartbroken.

The last year had been an emotional rollercoaster. My husband and I celebrated as we mailed our adoption application and cried when our homestudy was returned because it was signed in black ink instead of blue. We high-fived as each dossier document arrived on schedule and then sighed as we drove the two hours to our state's capital for the umpteenth time to replace a simple apostille stamp.

We poured every dime we owned into the adoption process, every ounce of strength into bringing a child home. We dreamed and prayed over a child we didn't know, hoping she was warm, healthy, and happy, but we had the stomach lurching fear she was really cold, sick, and afraid. And all the while, as we rumbled through the adoption process, we wondered which day was her birthday and prayed someone would make it special for her.

Now it was all over. Our dream was dead. After twenty-one long days of waiting in a foreign country, dozens of road-blocks, and two failed appointments with the Ukrainian government, we were at the end. If we wanted one last meeting with the adoption officials, we would have to wait in Kiev during the Christmas holidays. They wouldn't hand out new appointments until the middle of January and even then there was no guarantee they would see us. But leaving Kiev would shove us to the back of an already long line and honestly, we couldn't afford to come back.

We agonized over the decision. We sent up half-hearted prayers but never felt any peace. Finally, we called our travel agent. There was nothing more we could do. Staying in Kiev wasn't going to do us any good. We needed to fly out as soon as possible.

Her news wasn't any better. All the flights were booked. We were stuck.

Furious, I slammed down the phone and let my heavenly Father have it. Weren't we doing what He wanted us to do? How could He drag us half-way around the world on a wild goose chase? All the money we spent, the emotional energy we invested, the hearts I knew would be broken when we told our three other children the news. How could He let me love a child I would never know? I'd done everything He asked. On and on I went, my list of complaints growing by the minute.

"What more do you want from me, Lord?" I cried.

Exhausted, I fell on my face and sobbed. I lay there for what seemed like hours, spent. Then I did what God wanted me to do all along.

"Father," I whispered, my cheek pressed against the cold tile floor, "I'm tired of this roller coaster. It's all Yours. Take us home or work a miracle…whatever You want is fine."

A quiet peace filled me. Exhausted, I fell asleep.

The next morning we got a call. Our facilitator found a little girl in the southern part of the country, near the Black Sea. Did we want to meet her?

With no time to think, we jumped back on that roller coaster. But this time we held on to the roll bar with one hand, and downed a bottle of antacid with the other. Without so much as a name or a birthday to go on, we took off for Odessa. We were in the dark about what we would find, but that was okay. After all, God was in control.

Isn't it amazing how often we forget that simple lesson? How many times do we have to reach the breaking point before we learn our heavenly Father has our back?

The apostle Peter wrote in his first letter, "'God opposes the proud but favors the humble.' So humble yourselves under the mighty power of God, and at the right time he will lift you up in honor. Give all your worries and cares to God, for he cares about you." (1 Peter 5:5b–7)

It's not our tears God is after. Our heavenly Daddy hurts as much as we do when we face tough times. It's the broken and contrite spirit He needs. God is not going to step in where He isn't wanted. Unfortunately, we just get in the way of His perfect will when we try to handle things on our own.

But when we reach the end of ourselves, and turn everything over to our all-knowing and all-loving Abba Father, He will move. It requires letting go of our pride and leaning on Him, depending on Him, realizing He has the best possible outcome in mind for us. When we do that, He will give us peace and honor our sacrifice.

When I finally figured that out, when I humbled my heart and handed God all of the control, He gave my husband and me the desire He placed in our hearts.

Twenty-four hours after that phone call, we stood in an orphanage director's office in southern Ukraine as a beautiful, energetic, and intriguing little girl bounded into the room and straight into our hearts.

After more than 320 days of paper-chasing, waiting, praying and searching, we finally recognized God's hand in the whole process. His plan, His timing was perfect all along. We had finally found Ellie.

-Tamara Clymer

❦

"God opposes the proud but favors the humble.' So humble yourselves under the mighty power of God, and at the right time he will lift you up in honor. Give all your worries and cares to God, for he cares about you." — 1 Peter 5:5b–7

❦

Prayer

Father, when life seems out of control…when it seems like there is nothing left for me to do, remind me that You are there. Show me Your power and give me Your peace. Remind me that Your ways are perfect, and if I'll step back and allow You to work, in the end I'll be right where You want me to be. Amen.

Flight Delay

*"The LORD has made the heavens his throne; from
there he rules over everything." — Psalm 103:19*

My husband, two kids, and I were more than ready to
get home. After a great visit with my in-laws, it was
time. Being away from home is tough on toddlers.
They don't sleep well and you can almost forget about a schedule. We were ready to fly out of there.

So when we woke up that morning to a snow storm slam-
ming the St. Louis area, we were nervous. We waited, holding
our collective breaths, to learn the status of our flight. Finally
they announced: CANCELLED.

While we easily rescheduled our flight for the next day, I
will admit I was frustrated.

Doesn't God know how badly I want to get home? I thought.
And hubby has so much work to do.

That evening, about the time our plane would have taken
off, I got a call from my mother. My nephew had been in a terrible sledding accident. There were no details. She just knew he
was life-flighted to St. Louis' Children's Hospital. My mother,
who lives three hours away, was in tears.

"Can you drive there to be with your brother?" she cried.

I gathered my things, jumped in the car, drove slowly

through the snow, and arrived at the hospital forty-five minutes later. My nephew had just gone in for an MRI and my brother and sister-in-law were trying to find a way to get their three younger children to a sitter.

I saw the hand of God in every detail of that night. I sat with my sister-in-law as her son was brought back to the ICU and examined. And I prayed with them. My brother's family had just started attending church again. I was able to encourage my sister-in-law that God didn't do this to punish them, and while I didn't know why He allowed this to happen, I did know that God was all-powerful, the Great Physician. He always has a special place in His heart for the broken-hearted. He would work this all for His glory.

My nephew suffered three broken vertebrae and a cracked skull, but over time God healed his body with only a few side effects. As a result, my brother's family connected with their new church family quickly.

I've no doubt the God of the universe had a thousand reasons for sending a snow storm to St. Louis to cancel my flight. I feel blessed to have seen His mighty hand at work and to be there to encourage my family. Often times it is easy to focus on circumstances as inconveniences, when really, they are opportunities made for us by our Creator.

- Holly Hauskins

❧

"The disciples were amazed. 'Who is this man?' they asked. 'Even the winds and the waves obey him!'" — *Matthew 8:27*

Prayer

Thank You, God, for being in control of all things, including the weather. You reign over all. Thank You also for the opportunities we have to play a role in Your kingdom. Help us to trust that when our plans go awry, You are at work. Help us to look at all inconvenient circumstances in our lives as opportunities to be used by You. Amen.

Mercy

"The Lord is compassionate and merciful, slow to get angry and filled with unfailing love." — *Psalm 103:8*

Bike Accident

"The LORD is like a father to his children, tender and compassionate to those who fear him." — Psalm 103:13

I s God really tender and compassionate? I admit, there have been times when I've wondered. When life seems impossible to endure — family crisis, death of a loved one, betrayal by a friend — it is tough to find His mercy. But that's when I think back to a time several years ago when God allowed me to see Him as a tender and faithful father.

It was in the spring and though the sun was shining, it was quite chilly. I was driving through my hometown on a street I had traveled for over thirty years, when I realized I had made a wrong turn.

As I began to chide myself for such a silly mistake, I noticed a man pushing a small girl on her bicycle up the hill on the sidewalk. I remembered doing the same thing with my children. He was teaching his daughter how to ride a bike, but instead of sending her down the hill, he pushed her up.

How smart, I thought. If he pushed her downhill, she would crash.

I caught up to them just as he let go. For a moment, the little girl balanced and steered the bike on her own, so proud of herself. But seconds later, her smile turned to a look of pure terror. Her bike started wobbling and she lost control. Her quick-thinking dad grabbed her sweatshirt and held her up over the bike, like a tea bag over a cup of hot water — saving her from a painful crash.

I rounded the next corner and made my way back to my original route. But as I drove, I thought about how much that scene is like our Christian life. As we walk the path God has laid out for us, there are going be disasters along the way. Isaiah 41:10 says, "Do not be afraid, for I am with you. Don't be discouraged, for I am your God. I will strengthen you and help you. I will hold you up with my victorious right hand."

Sometimes we will be spared from disasters and sometimes we will have to go through them. But the promise is there. We are not alone. We have a wise heavenly Father by our side.

Just like the little girl's father pushed her uphill to keep her from riding faster than he knew she could handle, our heavenly Father allows us to be in situations he knows we can handle, if we will rely upon him.

That's where the "fear him" from Psalm 103:13 comes in. "The Lord is like a father to his children, tender and compassionate to those who fear him." In this case, fear means to honor him, be in awe of him.

How is it possible to honor him in times of crisis? We can honor him by believing his promises to us. As the old hymn says, we are to trust and obey and he will do the rest. He will not let us down, but rather just the opposite. He will strengthen us, help us, and uphold us just as he promised.

– Jonna Dingus

~~~~~~

*"Do not be afraid, for I am with you. Don't be discouraged,
for I am your God. I will strengthen you and help you. I will
hold you up with my victorious right hand." — Isaiah 41:10*

~~~~~~

Prayer

*Heavenly Father, help me to see all You are doing in my life, even
when it seems like a huge disaster. Help me to remember that
whatever is happening to me is no surprise to You. Instead, You
are with me every step of the way, carrying me. Thank You, Father,
for Your wisdom in not giving me more than what You will
handle in me as I trust in You. May I see this as an opportunity
to know You better and love You more deeply. Amen.*

The Climb

"But the love of the LORD remains forever with those who fear him." — Psalm 103:17a

God is a loving Father who has compassion on His children. He loves us and wants only what is best for us.

And just as our earthly dad keeps an eye on us, keeping us from getting hurt when we do things we shouldn't, our heavenly Father is always on guard. He often has to protect His children from physical and spiritual danger. I know of one particular time God literally kept my foot from slipping.

Our church's singles group was on a picnic at a Superior, Wisconsin, park. A stream ran through the middle of the place and had a rock cliff rising up on the other side. Someone spotted a sign laying at the edge of the water. Curious, we climbed down the steep slope to see what it said. We couldn't help laughing when we read, "WASHING CARS PROHIBITED."

As we started heading back, Karen, always up for an adventure, glanced up at that steep cliff and decided to climb it.

"Come on," she encouraged, "It will be fun."

Most of the others were wise enough not to take her challenge, but my roommate and I decided to give it a try.

We crossed the stream and looked up at the sheer rock cliff before us. It was steep! Undaunted, Karen started climbing.

She went a short distance and then called, "Come on, this is easy. There, to the right, is a toe-hold and just above it is one for your fingers."

My roommate followed her, feeling for the holds. I hesitated a bit, but then followed. All the way up, Karen told us where to find the toe and finger holds. And that's what they were, a bump on the rock just big enough to rest your big toe on and grab with the ends of your fingers so you could pull yourself up.

I was convinced we were never going to make it, but once I started there was no way to back out. I didn't dare look down, and didn't want to look up, so for the next twenty-five feet I kept my nose next to the cliff as I hunted for those elusive holds.

When we got to the top, our group was there to congratulate us. Then they told us some children died earlier that month when they fell while trying to scale the same cliff.

Does God protect us from the physical dangers in our life? I believe He does. But even more important, He protects us from spiritual dangers. How many times do we look for those elusive thrills and think they will make our life more exciting? "It won't hurt if I do it just this once", we tell ourselves when we're tempted to indulge in something we know is sin.

There are many temptations lurking out there, enticing us. God has promised He will forgive us when we sin, but we don't need to try His patience by going into areas and doing things we know we shouldn't.

Climbing the cliff that summer afternoon wasn't a sin, but I could have been another statistic that day. And I can end up a statistic of another sort when I willingly do things or go places I know are wrong.

As an earthly father looks out for his kids, so God will protect me from the dangers of this life that can result in sin. God does not prohibit me from doing what I want to do; He gives me free will to choose my actions.

But if I love Him with all of my heart, soul, and mind, He doesn't need to put signs everywhere telling me what I can and cannot do. If my heart is in tune with the Holy Spirit, I will have all I need to live a life that pleases Him.

- Delaine Swardstrom

※※※

"He will not let you stumble; the one who watches over you will not slumber." — Psalm 121:3

※※※

Prayer

Heavenly Father, thank You for watching out for me, in the physical area as well as the spiritual. Help me to keep my heart tuned to You, through Your Word, so I don't succumb to temptation. Amen.

Mercy, Grace, and a Breakdown

"The Lord is compassionate and merciful, slow to get angry and filled with unfailing love." — Psalm 103:8

I am always amazed at people who believe the God of the Old Testament was a mean-spirited, vindictive being just waiting to pounce on the unwary sinner and zap 'em with a lightning bolt!

There are verses all through Scripture that give us a glimpse at God's merciful nature. And I've seen it firsthand.

I was in my early twenties and had wandered away from God. My life was a mess. I had been running from God so hard and so long, I finally ended up bound to a hospital bed suffering from an emotional and mental breakdown.

Afraid I was a danger to myself and others, the hospital kept me in restraints because I was literally out of my mind. There in that hospital room, God sent His mercy to me in the form of a small, timid Baptist chaplain. Sitting on the edge of that bed, he began to tell me the simple story of a man who, out of love for me, died on a lonely hill called Calvary.

The pastor didn't know me. He didn't know I grew up in a

Christian home, going to church each week. He didn't know I could have told the story he shared with more panache and charisma, but for the first time I actually listened to the words.

Lying in that bed, strapped to the rails, tears poured down my face as I told God I didn't deserve to live because of the sins I'd committed. I deserved His wrath and anger at my disobedience and lifestyle.

As I confessed my sins to Him, I saw Christ walk in and stand at the foot of my bed. "Just let me die!" I cried out.

He just stretched out His hands and I saw the nail scars. "My son, I've already died so you don't have to." He smiled.

He'd already paid the debt I owed for my sins. He'd already cleared the slate and was willing to give me a second chance. By His mercies I was not consumed, but set free to live for Him. Oh, the mercies He poured out on me. I was forgiven!

God does not change. The same God who released me from my sin that day, is the same one who saved Adam and Eve from immediate death in the Garden of Eden. His mercy saved Noah and his family from the flood. It was His mercy that inspired the prophets to proclaim the coming of the Messiah. And His mercy bridges the gap sin created between God and His creation.

His merciful nature continues today. The Old Testament tells us, "The faithful love of the LORD never ends! His mercies never cease. Great is his faithfulness; his mercies begin afresh each morning." (Lam. 3:22–23) I love verse 22. We, who are devious and sinful, deserve to be consumed in the flames of hell, but His mercy reaches out to us to save us! His loving kindness provided the way to be restored to a right relationship with Him. His grace prompted him to give Jesus as the atoning sacrifice that would wash away the stain of sin and make us white as snow.

It was God's faithfulness that brought me back. Though I had done things that deserved His anger and wrath, He showed me

His mercies. Even though I'd failed Him, His compassion and grace were extended to me. He loved me enough to chase me down to the very depths of the ocean to express that love to me.

I am so grateful for that mercy.

– Wendon Pettey

⟡⟡⟡

"The faithful love of the LORD never ends!
His mercies never cease. Great is his faithfulness; his
mercies begin afresh each morning." — Lamentations 3:22–23

⟡⟡⟡

Prayer

Heavenly Father, I am a sinner, born in sin, raised in depravity, and worthy of eternal punishment. My sins are many, and I cannot pay the price to redeem them, or myself, in Your sight. But I claim the blood of Your Son, Jesus, that was shed on my behalf at Calvary. I believe He paid the price for my sins, and I accept Him as my Savior. I ask Him to be Lord of my life! Forgive me of my past and guide me daily from now on. Thank You, Lord, for saving my soul! Amen.

Contributors

DEBRA L. BUTTERFIELD is a freelance writer, editor, speaker, and writing coach, and an editor with Cross-River Media Group. Prior to freelancing, she worked for Focus on the Family as a junior copywriter. She the author of *Carried by Grace, Abba's Promise, Unshakable Faith* and has contributed to other projects. Debra enjoys the outdoors and has three adult children and two grandchildren. DebraLButterfield.com

TAMARA CLYMER is a publisher, Bible teacher, and author. Born and raised in the Midwest, she earned a journalism degree from Kansas State University. In 2010, she founded CrossRiver Media Group — a Christian publishing company. Tamara and her family live in western Kansas where they keep busy with sports, church, and summer camping trips to the mountains. — TamaraClymer.com

JONNA DINGUS is a wife and mother and retired from her job as her church's receptionist. She and her husband, Dan, have three grown children, two son-in-laws, and nine grandchildren. Jonna has been involved in women's ministries in her home church of Harmony Bible Church in Danville, Iowa, for many years. She enjoys Bible studies and encouraging and discipling younger women.

BARBARA GORDON lives with her husband of thirty-six years in a small town in west-central Missouri. They have three grown sons, their wives and two precious grandchildren. Barbara recently retired from a public school system where she was a district administrator. Her days are now filled with babysitting her grandchildren and her hobbies, which include reading, geocaching, and jogging.

SHANNA GROVES is the author of *Confessions of a Lip Reading Mom* and *Lip Reader*. In addition to speaking to groups, she has written for *Hearing Loss Magazine*, HealthyHearing.com, *The Kansas City Star*, *MOMSense* magazine and A Cup of Comfort books. A graduate of the University of Sciences and Arts of Oklahoma, Shanna holds a degree in communication. — LipreadingMom.com

MERRIE HANSEN and her husband have called seven different states home, but recently hit the road with tools, converted utility trailer, motorcycle, and their fifteen-year-old cat to serve Lord. Merrie writes devotionals to challenge, encourage, and inspire others. Merrie can be found Livin' Out Loud for Jesus at MerrieHansen.com or Facebook.com/MerrieHansen.

HOLLY HAUSKINS is a happy wife and stay-at-home mother in Helena, Montana. She holds a master's degree in English Education and enjoys spending time outdoors, traveling, reading, and experimenting in the kitchen. Holly is active in her local church and MOPS, has a passion for missions, and frequently speaks to groups of women, encouraging them to be authentic and content in their Christian walks.

ALYCIA HOLSTON is the author of *While the Giant is Sleeping*, a children's book that tells the story of the Sleeping Giant mountain of Helena, Montana, who slumbers while the world changes around him. Born and raised in the Midwest, Alycia earned her geography degree from Kansas State University. Alycia, her husband, and their three children live in Helena where they see the Sleeping Giant every day.

COLEEN JOHNSON writes and speaks from a depth that comes from personal loss and a decision to overcome. She speaks at women's retreats, seminars, conferences or groups. Coleen is a member of Ozark Christian Writers Group and speaks for Stonecroft Christian Women's International. She makes her home in Missouri.

RONALD JOHNSON is a freelance writer and published author. He is also retired from the Assemblies of God national offices in Springfield, Missouri. Besides writing, Ronald enjoys reading the Bible, studying theology books, as well as reading books on the American Civil War. He and his wife Gloria have one son, Christopher, a daughter-in law, Quillen, and three beautiful grandchildren.

DEB KEMPER is a freelance writer and poet hailing from northwest Florida. She now lives in Kansas City, Missouri, with her husband and two dogs. Her first novel, *Mallory Ridge* has received two awards. She is also working on two more novels. She belongs to Heart of America Christian Writers Network and Christian Writer's Fellowship. — DebKemper.com

PEGGY ANN KENNEDY lives in Wyoming with her high-school sweetheart, her husband of more than thirty-four years. She has written several articles for various e-zines, as well as contributing to other compilations, and has a self-published book of poetry. Peggy is also a contributing columnist for the *Laramie Daily Boomerang*'s religion page.

KAREN MAAG is a Christian speaker and writer from northwestern Missouri, who has a passion for women who are hurting and the friends and family who support them. She is a wife, mother, and grandmother of five and enjoys cooking, decorating, and sharing the message God has given her. — KarenMaag.com

ANGELA MEYER lives in Nebraska with her husband of twenty-six years and their high school daughter. Their older son has recently flown the nest. Angela enjoys the ocean, good stories, connecting with friends, taking pictures, quiet evenings, and a good laugh. On her someday-to-do list, she wants to vacation by the sea and ride in a hot air balloon. — AngelaDMeyer.com

CRYSTAL NICHOLS lives in a suburb of Kansas City, Missiouri, where she teaches middle school, is married to her best friend, and has two beautiful children. She also blogs about life with God, autism and special education issues, and shares things that amuse her and make her think. Crystal is the author of the book *Distant*. You can find her at CrystalANichols.com, or @ NicholsWriter on Twitter, Instagram, and Facebook.

WENDON PETTEY is a Roswell, New Mexico, native who retired to Alamogordo, New Mexico, where he ministers as an evangelist and Southern Gospel recording artist. He is working on his second Southern Gospel album and a devotional book for men. Recently widowed, he homeschools his two teenaged sons and is relearning how to run a household.

MARCIA SCHWARTZ is a retired English teacher whose poems, stories, and articles have appeared in various Christian magazines over the years. Her book of devotions, *Apples for the Soul,* is available on Amazon. Marcia and her husband, Hank, live in Nebraska and are the parents of two grown sons and a granddaughter. Marcia enjoys reading, writing, sewing, and tooling around in their little red Jeep.

PAMELA SONNENMOSER was an international speaker, author, and founder of Fresh Cup Ministries and Grace & Girlfriends Conferences. She was also the author of *Praise & Paraphrase, Beside the Empty Cradle,* and many more. Pamela was on the training faculty with CLASSeminars Inc., and she was a member of the Advanced Writers and Speakers Association (AWSA).

SHARON SPIEGEL has loved writing since she was a young girl. Now the Assembly of God minister, Christian school administrator, and self-described Missouri Yankee has added author to her titles. She is the author of *Generations* and the soon to be released *Anna.* She and her husband of more than forty years, Roger, have three children and fourteen grandchildren.

DELAINE SWARDSTROM is a registered nurse, who spent most of her career working in the correctional system. She and her husband, Jack, spent the first two years of their retirement in Germany as missionaries. She is the author of two novels, *Shattered Dreams* and *The Photograph.* Delaine and her husband have two grown children, five grandchildren, and one great-granddaughter.

RJ THESMAN is the author of the popular Reverend G trilogy published by CrossRiver Media, as well as *Sometimes They Forget - Finding Hope in the Alzheimer's Journey*. She enjoys teaching workshops, speaking at various venues, reading, gardening and cooking, especially anything with blueberries. You can follow RJ Thesman on Facebook, Twitter, LinkedIn and Goodreads. — RJThesman.net.

CATHERINE ULRICH-BRAKEFIELD is the author of inspirational historical fiction: *The Wind of Destiny*, *Wilted Dandelions*, and the first of a four book Destiny series, *Swept into Destiny*. She and her husband, Edward, have two adult children and three grandchildren. Their Arabian horses happily reside with them in Addison Township, Michigan. — CatherineUlrichBrakefield.com

CrossRiver

If you enjoyed this book, will you
consider sharing it with others?

- Please mention the book on Facebook, Twitter, Pinterest, or your blog.

- Recommend this book to your small group, book club, and workplace.

- Head over to Facebook.com/CrossRiverMedia, 'Like' the page and post a comment as to what you enjoyed the most.

- Pick up a copy for someone you know who would be challenged or encouraged by this message.

- Write a review on Amazon.com, BN.com, or Goodreads.com.

- To learn about our latest releases subscribe to our newsletter at CrossRiverMedia.com.

Abba's
PROMISE

33 Stories of God's Pledge to Provide

More great devotions from...
CROSSRIVERMEDIA.COM

UNBEATEN
Lindsey Bell

Difficult times often leave Christians searching the Bible for answers to the most difficult questions — Does God hear me when I pray? Why isn't He doing anything? Author Lindsey Bell understands the struggle. She searched the Bible for answers to these tough questions. Her studies led her through the stories of biblical figures, big and small. She discovered that while life brings trials, faith brings victory. And when we rely on God for the strength to get us through, we can emerge *Unbeaten*.

THE GRACE IMPACT
Nancy Kay Grace

The promise of grace pulses throughout Scripture. Chapter after chapter, the Bible shows a loving heavenly Father lavishing His grace on us through His Son. In her book, *The Grace Impact*, author Nancy Kay Grace gives us a closer glimpse at God's character. His grace covers every detail of life, not just the good things, but the difficult, sad and complicated things. That knowledge can give us the ability to walk confidently through life knowing God is with us every step of the way.

THIS I KNOW
Toby Holsinger

Author and teen, Tobi Holsinger, has discovered that while the Bible was written two thousand years ago, our heavenly Father has some great advice and insight on some of the toughest stuff teens face including rape, gossip, suicide, and peer pressure. Whatever you're facing, God understands and His Word holds answers, compassion. and encouragement. Grab your Bible and a pen and get ready to take a fresh look at God's Word. – (2014 CSP Book of the Year)

JOIN CROSSRIVER ONLINE...

CrossRiverMedia.com

Facebook.com/CrossRiverMedia

Twitter.com/CrossRiverMedia

Pinterest.com/CrossRiverMedia

Instagram.com/CrossRiverMedia